See It & Say It! Volume 1

First (1st) Grade Sight Words

Speedy Publishing LLC
40 E. Main St. #1156
Newark, DE 19711
www.speedypublishing.com

all all all all

Use it in a sentence.

an an an an

Use it in a sentence.

go

go go go go

Use it in a sentence.

my my my my

Use it in a sentence.

no

no no no no

Use it in a sentence.

be

be be be be

Use it in a sentence.

at at at at

Use it in a sentence.

sat

sat sat sat sat

Use it in a sentence.

yes

yes yes yes yes

Use it in a sentence.

are

are are are are

Use it in a sentence.

can

can can can can

Use it in a sentence.

had

had had had had

Use it in a sentence.

am am am am

Use it in a sentence.

into

into into into into

Use it in a sentence.

let

let let let let

Use it in a sentence.

day

day day day day

Use it in a sentence.

did

did did did did

Use it in a sentence.

has

has has has has

Use it in a sentence.

me

me me me me

Use it in a sentence.

little

little little little

Use it in a sentence.

big

big big big big

Use it in a sentence.

as as as as

Use it in a sentence.

see

see see see see

Use it in a sentence.

we we we we we

Use it in a sentence.

run

run run run run

Use it in a sentence.

was

was was was was

Use it in a sentence.

saw

saw saw saw saw

Use it in a sentence.

two

two two two two

Use it in a sentence.

too

too too too too

Use it in a sentence.

will will will will

Use it in a sentence.

ran

ran ran ran ran

Use it in a sentence.

this

this this this this

Use it in a sentence.

up

up up up up

Use it in a sentence.

down

down down down

Use it in a sentence.

on

on on on on

Use it in a sentence.

ask

ask ask ask ask

Use it in a sentence.

new

new new new new

Use it in a sentence.

old

old old old old

Use it in a sentence.

about

about about about

Use it in a sentence.

from

from from from

Use it in a sentence.

girl

girl girl girl girl

Use it in a sentence.

have

have have have

Use it in a sentence.

came

came came came

Use it in a sentence.

get

get get get get

Use it in a sentence.

off off off off

Use it in a sentence.

away away away

Use it in a sentence.

its

its its its its

Use it in a sentence.

by

by by by by

Use it in a sentence.

out

out out out out

Use it in a sentence.

sun

sun sun sun sun

Use it in a sentence.

they

they they they

Use it in a sentence.

not

not not not not

Use it in a sentence.

help

help help help help

Use it in a sentence.

his

his his his his

Use it in a sentence.

look

look look look

Use it in a sentence.

said

said said said said

Use it in a sentence.

way

way way way way

Use it in a sentence.

when when when

Use it in a sentence.

stop

stop stop stop

Use it in a sentence.

say

say say say say

Use it in a sentence.

thing

thing thing thing

Use it in a sentence.

what what what

Use it in a sentence.

put

put put put put

Use it in a sentence.

cat cat cat cat

Use it in a sentence.

dog

dog dog dog dog

Use it in a sentence.

men

men men men men

Use it in a sentence.

him

him him him him

Use it in a sentence.

but

but but but but

Use it in a sentence.

cry

cry cry cry cry

Use it in a sentence.

fun

fun fun fun fun

Use it in a sentence.

got

got got got got

Use it in a sentence.

bed

bed bed bed bed

Use it in a sentence.

were

were were were

Use it in a sentence.

with

with with with

Use it in a sentence.

sky

sky sky sky sky

Use it in a sentence.

pet

pet pet pet pet

Use it in a sentence.

room

room room room

Use it in a sentence.

very

very very very

Use it in a sentence.

tell

tell tell tell tell

Use it in a sentence.

why why why why

Use it in a sentence.

her

her her her her

Use it in a sentence.

fly

fly fly fly fly

Use it in a sentence.

hat

hat hat hat

Use it in a sentence.

now now now now

Use it in a sentence.

book

book book book

Use it in a sentence.

hello

hello hello hello

Use it in a sentence.

ball

ball ball ball ball

Use it in a sentence.

pig pig pig pig

Use it in a sentence.

tree

tree tree tree tree

Use it in a sentence.

stay

stay stay stay

Use it in a sentence.

so

so so so so

Use it in a sentence.

would

would would would

Use it in a sentence.

could

could could could

Use it in a sentence.

may may may may

Use it in a sentence.

aunt

aunt aunt aunt

Use it in a sentence.

know

know know know

Use it in a sentence.

miss

miss miss miss

Use it in a sentence.

best

best best best

Use it in a sentence.

car

car car car car

Use it in a sentence.

here

here here here

Use it in a sentence.

hill hill hill hill

Use it in a sentence.

eat

eat eat eat eat

Use it in a sentence.

apple

apple apple apple

Use it in a sentence.

Visit
BABY PROFESSOR
EDUCATION KIDS
www.BabyProfessorBooks.com
to download Free Baby Professor eBooks
and view our catalog of new and exciting
Children's Books

www.ingramcontent.com/pod-product-compliance
Lightning Source LLC
LaVergne TN
LVHW082248150826
845677LV00009B/1566

9798869448910